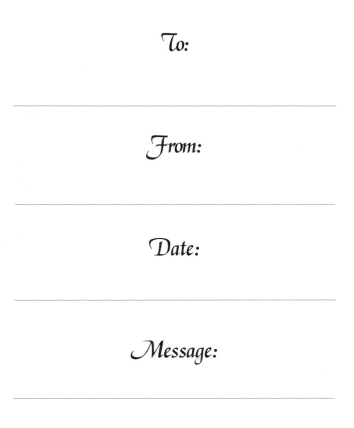

To:

From:

Date:

Message:

Light
Reflections

Alma Barkman

MOODY
The Name You Can Trust®
A MINISTRY OF MOODY BIBLE INSTITUTE

LIGHT REFLECTIONS by Alma Barkman

© 1999:   Christian Art
          PO Box 1599
          Vereeniging
          1930
          South Africa

This book was first published in the United States by Moody Press with the title of *Light Reflections*, copyright © 1990 by the Moody Bible Institute of Chicago.

Designed by: Christian Art

ISBN 08024-4755-4

Printed in Singapore.

Travel Trials

They wandered in the wilderness in a desert region; they did not find a way to an inhabited city. They were hungry and thirsty.
Psalm 107:4-5

$\mathcal{T}$ravel can be exhausting, especially when unexpected trials arise. I was aboard a DC-9 recently and the plane was bucking all over the sky, causing me to imagine that air pilots serve their apprenticeship at rodeos. Not the least perturbed, the captain calmly announced that we were experiencing "slight turbulence." Would we please tighten our seat belts?

Mine was already at the last notch. It had been such a long flight. I felt as if I had been galloping for hours over the Wild West. I can't stomach a full-course meal astride a bucking bronco, so I ride 'em hungry – so hungry my seat belt grates on my backbone.

At last a perceptive flight attendant noticed how drawn

6

and pale I looked and served a cold drink. Since the chuck wagon was so long overdue, the watering trough was a welcome sight. I grasped my cola, held it firmly between whitened knuckles, and raised it to my parched lips.

At that moment the wily old steed plunged headlong into an air pocket. It was all I could do to stay in the saddle. My soft drink was not so fortunate. It shot straight into the air and descended on my head in a hailstorm of ice cubes. Numb with shock, I sat staring into the empty cup for the duration of the flight.

Eventually we shuddered and pitched to a stop in front of an isolated airport. My bowed legs felt as though they would give way as I dismounted and headed for the oasis. I was getting closer and closer to that shimmering fountain made famous in Western song. Summoning my last ounce of strength, I bent over for a drink – and nearly stuck my nose into an ashtray.

It was a mirage of the most maddening sort.

It also illustrates how difficult it is to distinguish fact from fancy when we are overtired, upset, and thirsty. Yet life has its desert experiences, times when the smooth flight we may have expected suddenly becomes prolonged turbulence. Pitched and tossed about "by every wind of doctrine, by the trickery of men, by craftiness in deceitful scheming" (Ephesians 4:14), we can become so spiritually parched that we are attracted to anything that remotely promises to quench our desperate thirst for truth. It is also one reason vulnerable people mistakenly stick their noses into sects and cults whose teachings bear only faint resemblance to the living water of Scripture. They thus become victims of their own distorted thinking – or as Isaiah said of the idolater who had forsaken the true God: "He feeds on ashes; a deceived heart has turned him aside. And he cannot deliver himself" (Isaiah 44:20).

Light: "Whoever drinks of the water that I [Jesus] shall give him shall never thirst; but the water that I shall give him shall become in him a well of water springing up to eternal life" (John 4:14).

Reflection: Am I mistaking "ashes for water" by ignoring the truths of God's Word?

Noteworthy Endeavor

I have not found so great faith.
Matthew 8:10, KJV*

$\mathcal{I}$ hear him coming up the driveway at a slower pace than usual. When I open the door, I am face to face with a galvanized washtub supported by a pair of legs.

The sneakers look familiar.

"What on earth is that for?" I ask.

"It's the amplifier for my bass fiddle," echoes a voice from underneath the tub. "Let me in."

"Where on earth did you find it?"

Our ten-year-old-son plunks the washtub down in the middle of the kitchen floor. "The neighbors a block over had it in their garbage. They said I could take it. We had to make some kind of instrument for our musical project – remember?"

Seems as though I faintly recall ...

He raids his father's workshop for pliers and vice grip

and proceeds to remove the drain hose from the bottom of the tub. After all, a bass fiddle that boasts a crest on the side reading "Chicago Heights Duty Leakproof Construction doesn't require the added prestige of a red rubber hose clamped to its middle. And anyway, the violin maker has ideas of wedging a piece of kite string into the hole and securing the other end to a stick. Turn the tub upside down, prop it up on one edge with a brick to "let the music out," and pluck the kite string. *Voilà!* Music to the ears.

The day the musical project is due at school is exceptionally windy, and a gust catches the galvanized tub and nearly blows Junior off the driveway. In the interest of safety I decide to give him a hand.

As I enter the school with the tub, the brick, the broom, the ball of string, and my tousled young bass violinist in tow, I get the distinct impression that the music teacher is not terribly impressed. She is a pert young thing who has not fully grasped the musical creativity of ten year olds and appears crestfallen by the pile of noisemakers accumulating in the corner. I wonder who she was expecting? Itzhak Perlman playing a Stradivarius?

As we add our awkward contribution to the orchestra pit, it is obvious that the teacher's unrealistic expectations have in no way diminished the enthusiasm of her young charges. Quite the contrary! Back home at supper, our son raves about their afternoon concert with unprecedented delight.

I often think back to that odd assembly of instruments when I read Psalm 95:1: "Make a joyful noise to the rock of our salvation" (KJV). Often we have preconceived notions as to what brings glory to God, and anything that falls outside the prescribed boundaries is viewed with skepticism, if not utter disdain. And yet the most joyful Christians are often those whose enthusiasm compensates for their lack of ability, and whose spontaneous creativity is far more delightful than rigid conformity.

Light: "With God all things are possible" (Matthew 19:26).

Reflection: Am I encouraging and utilizing those unique gifts and talents that could honor and glorify God?

* *King James Version.*

The Handwriting
on the Wall

The words of wise men are like goads.
Ecclesiastes 12:11

In my childhood there was no greater incentive to learning than a freshly washed blackboard on which snow-white chalk outlined our lessons in an authoritative hand. Every day a fresh challenge appeared in black and white, and it spurred me on to greater heights of achievement.

But there was another corner of the blackboard that goaded me – not to academic excellence but to moral rectitude. Reserved for the teacher's use, that corner of the blackboard chalked up a list of offenders daily. Rather than taking time to administer punishment at the moment of the misdemeanor, my teacher jotted down the names of the accused. Suffice it to say that suspects disputed her judgment at their peril.

The names remained on the blackboard for the duration of the day, or even the week, depending upon the severity and frequency of misconduct. Woe betide any transgressor who was caught erasing his own name, and pity the slanderer who added his enemy to the list! Such deletions and additions were made at the sole discretion of my teacher.

I can remember the fateful day when my name appeared among the accused. I was a first-time offender, and when the moment of reckoning came, I was in agony. What kind of punishment would be meted out? *Hard labor?* I could picture myself writing lines for days on end. *Incarceration?* Maybe I would have to forfeit recesses for the duration of the year. *Lashes?* I nearly fainted at the thought! My only recourse was to silently plead for mercy.

My teacher scrutinized my face, searching for evidence of repentance. After what seemed an eternity, she turned to the list of names. While I waited in fearful suspense, she made her decision. With a merciful smile, and a stroke of the eraser, my name was wiped away! I was forgiven! Exonerated! Acquitted! Set *free!*

The experience had such a profound effect on me that it altered my behavior for the entire term. I never again looked at that list of offenders without remembering the foreboding fear of punishment followed by the ecstasy of absolute forgiveness. Such is the power of the written word.

Just as my wise teacher kept before us a reminder of her authority both to punish and to forgive, so the written Word of God holds the power to condemn the rebellious yet restore the contrite to a right relationship with God. Lovingly scrutinizing our hearts, God longs to free us from the bondage of sin. "Repent therefore and return, that your sins may be wiped away, in order that times of refreshing may come from the presence of the Lord" (Acts 3:19). Only as we cast ourselves upon the mercies of God can we be forgiven! Exonerated! Acquitted! Set *free!*

Light: "I, even I, am the one who wipes out your transgressions for My own sake; and I will not remember your sins" (Isaiah 43:25).

Reflection: Do I use my liberty as a license to sin, or does genuine gratitude for God's forgiveness goad me to obedience?

Bread Delivery

*All the bread of their provision
was dry and had become crumbled.
Joshua 9:5*

$\mathcal{M}$uch to my frustration, Junior had reached that stage of development where a school bag was considered excess baggage. Any notes from his teacher were jammed into the pockets of his jeans and forgotten. On washday it usually took me an hour to read the backlog of information, most of it already outdated.

That's how I came to rely on the neighbors to keep me abreast of current events at school. It's also how I learned about the annual school tea to be held the next day – only this year it was not just a tea. It was to be a full-fledged bazaar featuring houseplants, handicrafts, white elephants, and a bake table.

Now you can't root a geranium in one evening, much less wrestle a white elephant from a family of compulsive

15

hoarders. What was I to send as my contribution? Some homemade bread perhaps?

Junior seemed receptive to the idea, so early the next morning I mixed up a batch of bread, and at noon I packaged two nicely shaped loaves for the bake table and put them in a bag. Junior was nonchalant as I exhorted him to be careful about how he handled them. In fact I had the feeling I should deliver the bread myself, but he was adamant.

"Good grief, Mom! Can't a guy be trusted?"

I wondered.

A mother's intuition is seldom wrong. It seemed Junior was halfway to school when the bag of bread got caught in the spokes of his bicycle. Before he could free it, the loaves were so mangled he brought them home in hopes there might be a possibility of salvaging the crumbs.

It was a good thing I had more bread to replace it. This time Junior was far more careful.

That incident raised a nagging question in terms of my own Christian walk. Could someone who neglected the message be counted upon to deliver the goods? Of late my personal Bible study was done in bits and snatches, jammed in among a dozen other tasks and frequently overlooked altogether. More and more I found myself relying on the teachings of others – on word-of-mouth knowledge.

The crunch came when a group of women asked me to lead a neighborhood Bible study. The bread of life

(John 6:35) I was trying to convey soon got caught in the twists and turns of lively discussions, and I realized I had nothing more to offer than scattered crumbs of Bible knowledge. Confessing my neglect, I set about salvaging the many wasted minutes of my day, and Bible study once again became a priority.

Light: "And He humbled you and let you be hungry ... that He might make you understand that man does not live by bread alone, but man lives by everything that proceeds out of the mouth of the Lord" (Deuteronomy 8:3).

Reflection: Am I making a conscious effort to gain fresh insights into God's Word so that I can deliver His truth to others at opportune times?

A Bird Feeder?

The seed is the word.
Luke 8:11

A blue jay, by nature, is a glutton. A magnificent bird, yes, but a glutton. He can clean out a bird feeder in the time it takes for a sparrow to return thanks. He swoops into a feeder, gobbles up everything, and squawks for more. Such an irritable disposition at mealtime would in itself be sufficient reason for ulcers, but the blue jay who dominates my birdfeeder has even further reason to be aggravated.

My tomcat keeps him under constant surveillance. Every time wings flutter on the horizon, Sir Purrcival Van Mouser comes stiffly to attention. Should the jay catch him at ease, his reaction is immediate and swift: an enormous leap, a wild gallop down the hall, and Purrvess is at his post. I fear one day his brakes may fail, and he will crash through the window. At present, however, he displays magnificent restraint, for which the blue jay should be thankful. But instead, the jay is indignant that a tomcat has the audacity to peer at him through the glass.

And yet for all his faults of gluttony, ingratitude, and irritability (or perhaps because of them) I can identify with that blue jay. Flying hither and thither in the course of the day's work, I can swoop into Scripture and skim a whole chapter in the time it takes for a scholar to collect his thoughts. Such a superficial approach toward the Word reveals an ungrateful attitude that can in itself be a serious hindrance to in-depth Bible study. But even more frightening is the thought that while I hastily gobble up snatches of Scripture here, there, and everywhere, my "adversary, the devil, prowls about like a roaring lion seeking someone to devour" (1 Peter 5:8). The more brilliant my spiritual "plumage", the greater his efforts to thwart my digestion of Scripture.

What the blue jay and I must both learn is that the *presence* of the enemy does not mean he will *prevail*. The tomcat may lick his chops in anticipation of blue jay brisket, but he is helpless to inflict any harm because the feeder is beyond his reach. So long as the blue jay exercises diligence and care, he receives both protection and nourishment.

In my case, the seed is the Word of God, and while Satan may lie in wait to catch me, claw at my inconsistencies, or pounce on my mistakes, his threatening demeanor is but a futile threat so long as I prayerfully appropriate scriptural truths on a daily basis. Contrary to what Satan may expect, the close scrutiny of his evil eye simply promotes a more careful walk, encourages a more disciplined life-style and calls me to complete reliance upon God. Engrossed in His Word, I am both fortified and fed.

Light: "How blessed is the man who does not walk in the counsel of the wicked, nor stand in the path of sinners, nor sit in the seat of scoffers! But his delight is in the law of the Lord, and in His law he meditates day and night" (Psalm 1:1-2).

Reflection: Despite the presence of evil around me, am I still determined to feed on God's Word?

Take Note

When he came and approached the
house, he heard music and dancing.
Luke 15:25

We first surmised our son's musical inclinations when he started shaking his baby rattle in a Latin American beat about one o'clock in the morning. When we deprived him of that amusement, he promptly banged his feet against the crib until it sounded like the roll of a kettledrum at the start of a rousing overture. In the morning we discovered the crib has been jiggled all night in time to a quick march, and the screws were rolling out the door to meet us. Meanwhile the toothless conductor in diapers was grinning out at us from his podium behind bars.

From the time he learned to walk, all roads led past the piano. No matter how early, how late, how casual, or how urgent his trip, he always reached up to execute a quick rendition of "plinkety, plank, plink." Ours was the only piano in the neighborhood with teething biscuits wedged between the keys. Close the piano, and there was a cupboard full of pots and pans to rattle and bang while mother was on the phone. And if church was a little too quiet, he might dance a little jig in the center aisle to loosen up the saints.

But musical spontaneity all too soon gave way to the aggravating age of shyness. Conscripted as the key soloist in a kindergarten production, our musical genius stood looking cross-eyed into the microphone and never sang a note, while children of lesser ability boldly warbled off-key.

In the end, the musical growth of a gifted child is no easier to predict than his spiritual walk. Although Scripture plainly tells us to bring up our children "in the nurture and admonition" of the Lord (Ephesians 6:4, KJV), there is no guarantee that Sunday school lessons will make him a believer any more than music lessons will make him a performer. Just as there are parents who have invested thousands of dollars in training a gifted child, only to have him turn his back on music, so there are Christians who have diligently trained their offspring in the faith, only to have him reject Christ.

Although disheartened, such parents can take comfort in the fact that they have been obedient to God's word. Early training is never altogether lost. Just as a pause in music does not indicate the end of a song, so an interval of indifference need not spell despair. Spiritual truths that fall on the deaf ears of youth are often reviewed with deep appreciation at an older age.

Light: "Train up a child in the way he should go, even when he is old he will not depart from it" (Proverbs 22:6).

Reflection: Do I pray daily for God to bring the lives of wayward children back into harmony with Him?

A Divine Decree

*And this was a small thing in Thine eyes, O
God; but Thou ... hast regarded me according
to the standards of a man of high degree.*
1 Chronicles 17:17

Every time I walk into a doctor's office the first thing I
notice is the noble certificate proclaiming the medicine
man's achievements. The fact that his diplomas are
written in Latin is of no reassurance to me whatsoever.
For all I know he may have earned his credentials
eviscerating poultry at the local meat packer's. But the
public at large accepts him as a qualified doctor because
he has the papers to prove it.

Even though a gastronomical disaster can be just as
damaging as the slip of a scalpel, my professional status
as a cook goes virtually unrecognized for want of the
proper documents. The Blue Ribbon people once
bolstered my sagging ego when I won a baking contest.

They sent me a certificate "suitable for framing." They could at least have printed it in Latin. For some reason visitors are not all that impressed by the fact that I had the best baking powder biscuits in the local county fair in 1967.

Raising a robust family would not have given me a chance to sit back and rest on my laurels anyway. Every time I put my feet up they cried, "I'm hungry!" or, "What's for supper?" Professionally speaking, I never did obtain proper credentials, but I've managed to fill the position of family chef for more than thirty years.

In retrospect I am thankful that feeding the hungry, clothing the naked, and visiting the sick are not prestigiously linked to diplomas, degrees, or documents, for then I could easily justify doing nothing. But God has chosen to work through me, not around me, so I have no excuse for standing in His way, feeling inadequate.

But isn't that the reason most of us give when we are asked to do something? Part of the problem is the fact that the world places great emphasis and value on theoretical knowledge as opposed to practical experience. Those of us with comparatively little education by way of formal training, therefore, struggle with feelings of intimidation and inferiority, both of which tend to stifle our full potential.

I must constantly remind myself that God puts priority on a spirit of servanthood. When James and John sought the promise of special recognition in glory, Jesus took the opportunity to point out one of the great distinctions of the Christian faith: "Whoever wishes to become great among you shall be your servant; and whoever wishes to be first among you shall be slave of all. For even the Son of Man did not come to be served, but to serve, and to give His life a ransom for many" (Mark 10:43-45).

Light: "Be strong and do not lose courage, for there is reward for your work" (2 Chronicles 15:7).

Reflection: Am I thinking too much about my inadequacies as God's servant and too little about the Person I serve? "I can do all things through Him who strengthens me" (Philippians 4:13).

Ups and Downs

The small as well as the great,
the teacher as well as the pupil.
1 Chronicles 25:8

$\mathcal{G}$etting younger children ready for another school term is like outfitting a mountain climber from scratch. I start at the bottom of the list and work my way up, the crowning achievement being the first day of school, when Junior skips down the road in stiff new jeans and bright yellow T-shirt, his shiny red school bag bulging with scholastic necessities.

He insists that everything be meticulously labeled, otherwise the slick talker in the next row might raise the question of ownership and lay claim to the owl-shaped eraser or the bright orange pencil. The loss of such valuables at the very outset of the term could conceivably undermine a young fellow's enthusiasm for school, which at present is at an all-time high.

In direct contrast, his teenage brother shuffles out the door wearing run-down sneakers and last year's jeans, a well-chewed pencil protruding from his hind pocket. Under one arm is a warped binder in which a half dozen loose-leaf papers flutter. He mumbles something about school being a waste of time, teachers being slave drivers, and compulsory education being a holdover from the Dark Ages. In other words, he has slipped from the peak of enjoyment to the valley of despair, not exactly an unusual experience during the learning process.

And where do I stand in *my* Christian pilgrimage? Elated by my shiny new robe of forgiveness and a brand-new supply of God's promises, am I still on the mountaintop of experience, naively unaware that along with certain God-given privileges come the added responsibilities of growth and learning and self-control? People in spiritual kindergarten must eventually be transformed by the renewing of their minds (Romans 12:2) to the Teacher's expectations. For some, it is a difficult course.

Or, like my high schooler, am I bogged down by the boredom of daily routine, having lost my incentive for Bible study, fellowship, and prayer? Am I ill equipped to meet the problems life poses? Maybe I even secretly grumble that study of Scripture is a waste of time, that preachers are boring, and that church is nothing but a traditional institution of the past.

As children of God, it is not unusual for us to slip from a mood of joyful anticipation to an attitude of dogged perseverance. That is a common reaction to the learning process. Whether we boast the crown of a brand new believer or bear the cross of a jaded Christian, however, we are not exempt from those disciplines even Christ deemed necessary. Service, prayer, meditation, and fellowship can rekindle the enthusiasm and change the daily outlook of everyone from the babe in Christ to the spiritually mature.

Light: "I will instruct you and teach you in the way which you should go; I will counsel you with My eye upon you" (Psalm 32:8).

Reflection: Am I learning that faith is not based on feelings, but that Christian maturity comes only through applying myself to those disciplines Christ illustrated in His exemplary life?

Staying Secure

For we brought nothing into this world,
and it is certain we can carry nothing out.
1 Timothy 6:7

$\mathscr{A}$ woman develops a strong attachment to her handbag. That is why you will see a woman carrying one even under the most unusual circumstances.

Go down to the docks in fishing season and watch the veteran mariners prepare for a day's fishing. If a woman is there, she will likely have her handbag in one hand and a rod and reel in the other. If not, she has already stowed it away in the forecastle, along with a fresh supply of hooks, two hundred feet of line, and a pair of scissors.

Or visit the local hospital. In the emergency room among the intravenous equipment, the oxygen tanks, and the bottles of blood plasma is a lady's handbag, placed within easy reach of its owner in case she needs a tissue.

Or attend the community picnic and get a front seat

on the grass in time for the ladies' race. Ten chances to one Grandma will not even place because she insists on toting her oversize handbag to the finish line.

Why does a woman choose to be thus handicapped for life? It is because she lives in constant fear of losing her purse. Next to the morbid thought of a kidnapper abducting her children is the haunting thought of someone stealing her handbag. It is all rather ridiculous, as any man will tell you, but it *could* happen, as every woman knows.

Although we all have many things in common, there is usually one aspect of life I look upon as "my bag." It might be a special talent I have, a position I hold, my job, a stylish wardrobe, a beautiful home. Whatever it is, I would feel lost without it. Such a strong dependency on outside resources creates its own underlying anxiety: What if my "bag" is snatched away and I lose my sense of identity? So I cling to it more than ever.

But sometimes when I think I am really going places, God stops me. Perhaps my conscience is pricked by a sermon on stumbling blocks, or I see my own selfishness in terms of world needs, or I am brought face to face with my priorities in the light of eternity. Then, like a passenger being checked by a security guard at an airline terminal, I wait in God's presence while He searches my "bag" for things that could pose a threat to my Christian progress. With reluctant obedience I yield them to His will, confident that He withholds only that which could endanger my spiritual journey.

Light: "For the Lord God is a sun and shield; the Lord gives grace and glory; no good thing does He withhold from those who walk uprightly" (Psalm 84:11).

Reflection: Can I accept the fact that the sacrifices God asks me to make are either for my spiritual welfare or for the benefit of others? Am I being conscientious in terms of my stewardship of spiritual gifts, time, talents, and possessions?

Appearances Can Be Deceiving

When they measure themselves by themselves,
and compare themselves with themselves,
they are without understanding.
2 Corinthians 10:12

"Different" is a dirty word to an adolescent. He could have a purple nose, spaghetti arms, and be three feet tall, but as long as the other kids were the same, he'd be perfectly happy. But let him get the idea that he is an inch shorter, a pound heavier, or a point sharper than the rest, and he immediately looks upon himself as an outcast.

The only solution, as he sees it, is to stretch, diet, or studiously avoid homework in hopes that he will either grow, lose weight, or receive lower marks. While going through this self-imposed regimen he is the picture of

33

abject misery. His muscles ache, he refuses to eat anything you set before him, and his conscience plagues him from one unfinished assignment to the next. And just when he thinks he has achieved his desired goal, he finds – to his utter horror – that he has a pimple on his chin. Or a mole on his back. Or a wart on his stomach.

Our neighbor tells me her son was so distraught because his little toe was crooked that he went to unbelievable lengths to correct it, including an appointment with a top orthopedic surgeon. The fact that the good surgeon told him to go home and not worry about it only aggravated his obsession with it. Here he was, at thirteen years of age, stuck with a toe so badly deformed that a top specialist wouldn't even touch it!

In a last desperate effort to straighten the offending toe, he tied a string around it every night and secured it to his bedpost. Afraid that his circulation might be so severely restricted the toe would drop off, his mother would wait until he was asleep and go in and untie the string.

This nightly ritual finally came to an end the day her son looked in the mirror and concluded that he never, *ever* would be one of the gang.

He didn't even have a moustache yet.

The emphasis in today's world on physical appearance has no doubt created inferiority complexes in a great many people, and some have gone to extreme lengths to correct what may actually be only slight variations from the norm. For those who are sensitive about some aspect of their appearance, however, it may be of comfort to know that even the Son of God Himself had "no stately form or majesty that we should look upon Him, nor appearance that we should be attracted to Him. He was despised and forsaken of men" (Isaiah 53:2-3). He knew the terrible pain of rejection and was "like one from whom men hide their face" (v. 3).

If we seek comfort and understanding during periods of alienation, it will not come through comparing ourselves to others but by turning in faith to the One who has experienced our anguish. Whatever blemishes or flaws we suffer physically, however, "a broken and a contrite heart, O God, Thou wilt not despise" (Psalm 51:17).

Light: "Great is our Lord, and abundant in strength; His understanding is infinite. The Lord supports the afflicted" (Psalm 147:5-6).

Reflection: Have I forgotten that man looks only on the outward appearance but God looks on the heart?

Dogged Resistance

My son, if sinners entice you, do not consent.
Proverbs 1:10

As I look out my window I can see two mongrels enjoying a picnic in somebody's garbage cans, and they have strewn the contents all across the road. Elated with their find, they show utter disdain for the conservative old canine who steadfastly observes them from the end of the adjacent driveway. He faithfully guards his master's house, including the garbage cans that sit before him.

As he watches the young rebels in the midst of their enjoyment, however, the old veteran's tongue periodically sweeps across his gray muzzle. Ah! What he wouldn't give for one of those forbidden bones. The old dog rises from his haunches and wags his tail hopefully, but the young mongrels pay no heed. It is so tempting to go over and help himself, but no! Duty calls, and the old dog lies down once more and rests his nose between his paws. This bit about being man's best friend evidently has its drawbacks, especially during moments of strong temptation.

The old dog rests with eyes closed. Better not to look than risk his reputation, although once in a while he steals a peek. Now that bone right over there, for instance ... If he could quickly snatch it and run, he could bury it behind the ...

His thoughts are interrupted by a garbage truck rumbling down the street. The old dog raises his ears in keen anticipation. The two culprits flee in terror, leaving behind the unsightly remains of two overturned garbage cans. The refuse collector, shaking his head in disgust, scoops up the scattered garbage as best he can and moves on.

Approaching Old Faithful, he playfully ruffles the dog's fur, commendig him for a job well done. Giving a great snort of satisfaction, the old dog turns and trots lightly to the house, where sleep is sweet because forbidden bones are not buried in his canine conscience.

Whether in dog or man, temptations are a test of faithfulness to the Master. All around us are those who take great pleasure in flouting ethical and moral standards, preferring to indulge in the very garbage that Scripture tells us to refuse. In Paul's farewell to the Ephesians, he warned them: "Be on guard for yourselves and for all the flock. ... Savage wolves will come in among you ... and from among your own selves men will arise, speaking perverse things, to draw away the disciples after them" (Acts 20:28-30).

Lured by those with similar professions of faith, it is especially difficult to resist temptation. "But everybody's doing it!" seems to imply a certain justification. It does not give us sufficient grounds to indulge, however. Paul reminded the elders at Ephesus of his own example of integrity as well as the responsibility they had as overseers of the church to "be on guard" for those whose lifestyle deserved admonishment, not adherents.

Light: "Blessed is the man who listens to me, watching daily at my gates, waiting at my doorposts" (Proverbs 8:34).

Reflection: Am I exercising wisdom and discernment to guard carefully those truths and principles that are most vulnerable to abuse in my own life?

Meeting the Teacher

*Your eyes will behold your Teacher. And your ears
will hear a word behind you, "This is the way, walk
in it," whenever you turn to the right or to the left."
Isaiah 30:20-21*

Every school term Junior comes through the door
clutching a Xeroxed sheet requesting another parent-
teacher interview. The importance of it is so indelibly
etched on his mind that his face is ashen white from the
mere responsibility of carrying it home. To his way of
thinking, the situation could not be more serious if the
town cop issued a warrant for my arrest.

From *my* viewpoint, it's always more like being called
up for jury duty. The teacher opens a massive file on the
accused, and I wonder how anyone could accumulate
that much information on a third grader. Suspicions are
leveled with cool objectivity and supported by a set of
evidence that would rattle a statistician.

There I sit, trying to weigh matters with strict impartiality, all the while hampered by ten years of total involvement with the suspect. How could I not be biased in favor of someone I have carried for nine months, for whom I have washed dozens of diapers, chased hundreds of preschool miles, and who resembles the man I love? My maternal instincts want to spring to his defense, but I dutifully listen to all the charges, mutely nodding my head in humble acceptance of the facts.

I have yet to figure out how a teacher who seems to spend half as much effort on my offspring knows twice as much about him, but I would be a foolish parent indeed to ignore the information before me just because I *feel* this way or *think* that way. Wisdom demands that I listen carefully to the teacher's assessment of our son's shortcomings so I can take the necessary measures to help him improve his learning skills.

The benefits are hard to weigh, much less appreciate, but such an interview gives me a sense of direction. Whenever I am called upon to help Junior with his homework, the teacher's expectations and honest advice hover in the background, guiding me through the problem areas.

The Holy Spirit's work is much the same. At some point in our lives God arrests our attention with an invitation to meet Him in a personal way. As He convicts us of our shortcomings, it is difficult for us as finite human beings to believe that a God whom we neither see nor hear nevertheless knows so much about us, but when we open His Book, there is no denying the insight He has into human nature.

Foolishness would tempt us to make vain excuses in our defense based on emotion or intellect. Wisdom ordains that we humbly acknowledge God's assessment of our spiritual condition and accept Him by faith in Jesus Christ. As we do, we find that life takes on a sense of purpose, because thereafter we have the advantage of His guidance through the Spirit of God that indwells us. As we draw upon His wisdom, we become conscious of His presence in every area of life – His expectations helping us determine our value system and His infinite knowledge giving us direction.

Light: "But the Helper, the Holy Spirit, whom the Father will send in My name, He will teach you all things, and bring to your remembrance all that I said to you" (John 14:26).

Reflection: Am I so biased in my own opinions that I ignore the promptings of God's Spirit as He seeks to lead me?

A Desire for Change

Why do you go around so much changing your way?
Jeremiah 2:36

When it comes to rearranging the furniture, I could put the refrigerator in the front room, the piano on the back porch, and stand the bed on end. The discovery would be acknowledged at best by a perfunctory grunt.

Moving the kitchen table, however, initiates response of a different sort. Friend hubby, you see, has presided over mealtime from his accustomed place for close to thirty years. The family has simply rotated around him according to age, behavior, and eating habits.

Yesterday I thought I needed a change. I took out the extension board and placed the shortened table crossways under the kitchen window.

"What is this anyway? The table has shrunk!"

"So has the family," I reminded him. "I took the extension out to give me more space in the kitchen."

42

He looked at the bare floor with disdain. "You always had enough room before."

"Well now I'll have a bit more."

My satisfaction was short-lived. I didn't receive my customary kiss on the cheek for being cook because friend hubby now sat too far away. The teenagers discovered they could elbow each other from different vantage points. I couldn't get up, down, and over to the stove the dozen or so times it takes to serve a meal. And even if all the logistics could have been ironed out, I would still be aware of one unalterable fact: there was no way to camouflage the four dents in the floor where the table legs have stood for thirty years.

Someone has said that there is nothing as permanent as change. We like to try new ideas, introduce new trends, experiment with the latest equipment. The human intellect has such an insatiable thirst to explore new dimensions for living that every innovative idea is hailed as progress.

Along with those ideas come the encumbent adjustments. And like moving the kitchen table, not all of them produce positive results. For instance, pushing aside the moral standards for fidelity set down in God's Word thwarts the close personal relationship He intended between husband and wife. Shoving aside biblical principles for disciplining children hinders good behavior. And twisting Scripture around in order to justify personal "freedom" gives more room to sin.

Should a professing Christian claim to enjoy the space thus created, his satisfaction is usually short-lived. He can never quite overlook the "indentations" of God's truth that have been indelibly impressed upon his conscience, and the burden of guilt will weigh heavily upon him until the Bible is reinstated to its proper place in his life. "For the word of God is living and active and sharper than any two-edged sword, and piercing as far as the division of soul and spirit, of both joints and marrow, and able to judge the thoughts and intentions of the heart" (Hebrews 4:12).

Light: "The grass withers, the flower fades, but the word of our God stands forever" (Isaiah 40:8).

Reflection: Are the changes I plan to make in my life in keeping with God's Word and His will?

In a Pickle

*And the rabble who were among them had greedy
desires ... and said, ... "We remember the cucumbers.*
Numbers 11:5

I try to prolong the pickling season as long as possible,
but eventually frost comes. I awaken one morning to
discover wilted brown leaves collapsed like miniature
tents over a skeleton framework of cucumber vines.

That's when the imposters show up. Stripped of their
protective foliage, they stand out like bloated goldfish –
great swollen cucumbers that have sapped more than
their share of nourishment from the vine, yet have the
audacity to hang on anyway. How they dodged the pickle
brine is beyond me, but there they are, and "jolly big
blokes at that" remarks my English friend. Of what use
are they now except to perpetuate their kind? And who
wants a race of fat yellow cucumbers usurping choice
gardening space? They are "good for nothing, but to be

45

cast out" (Matthew 5:13, KJV).

Yet lurking everywhere in the cucumber patch of human endeavor, we find similar freeloaders, contributing little, sapping much. Should the social structures that conceal them suddenly collapse, they would stand out as naked as ripe cucumbers after the first frost.

Closer to home, what about my little corner of God's vineyard? Do I want all the benefits but none of the sacrifices? Greedy desires can thrive amazingly well in the warm climate of Christian love, and even a bloated ego is frequently overlooked in the name of kindness. Given the chance, do I try to evade certain menial responsibilities because I feel such service is beneath someone of my spiritual stature? Or am I willing to be picked by God to fulfill His purposes, however small?

I wonder.

Do we dread the thought of sudden change, not for what it would destroy, but for what it could *reveal?* If our motives were subjected to the cold harsh scrutiny of an unforgiving climate instead of sheltered in a supportive framework, would we stand out naked and ashamed?

"The eyes of the Lord are in every place, watching the evil and the good" (Proverbs 15:3). Although it may not be immediately apparent to those around us, God is not deceived by underhanded motives. If our sole aim is to personally benefit from our involvement in God's vineyard, with little or no intention of serving others,

God may deal with us as He dealt with the greedy children of Israel. "He gave them their request, but sent leanness into their soul" (Psalm 106:15, KJV).

The picture is all too familiar – "jolly big blokes" who are hollow on the inside. Instead of growing in grace, they have become victims of their own greed, all the while hiding under the protective camouflage of Christianity. As believers, therefore, we have a twofold responsibility. First, we must not compromise personal integrity, no matter how tempting the returns. Second, we must expose impostors for what they really are.

Light: "And what does the Lord require of you but to do justice, to love kindness and to walk humbly with your God?" (Micah 6:8).

Reflection: Do I have a tangled perception of what really constitutes God's will for my life? Perhaps I need to remind myself that as a child of the King, I do not have to sap human resources for my sense of identity and self-worth.

Quality Control

You will know them by their fruits.
Matthew 7:16

$\mathcal{A}$t one time it was something of a novelty to discover huge hirsute peaches packed under a West Coast fruit label. The fuzz was so thick my jaws clung together from the drag, but there was flavor under all that fuzz – sweet tantalizing peach juice flooding my taste buds and dribbling down both arms. My mother recognized the telltale trickle as a sure sign that I had eaten from the forbidden fruit she intended to preserve.

Nowadays I open a box of peaches to find smooth defuzzed runts, pale facsimiles of the real thing. The slippery little slices go sliding down my throat before I even realize I am eating a peach.

Jsut think about it. Henceforth teenage boys will not know what I mean when I refer to the forerunner of the beard as "peach fuzz." And tongue in cheek, I will have to stop and explain all about God's intentions before the extremists took over the fruit orchards and degendered the peaches in one fell swoop of a genetic razor.

My teenager may pale considerably at the thought, and I will have to point out that there are radicals in all walks of life, tares in every field, thorns in every vineyard. Feminists, chauvinists, rebels, legalists, libertines, fanatics, heretics – there are so many seeds of discord being sowed by evil while the righteous sleep (Matthew 13:25).

Suddenly awakened from my usual state of apathy, my first reaction is to fight back. Uproot! Destroy! Eradicate the weeds!

But God says, "Wait a minute. You can't be angry, resentful, irritated, hasty, mean, vicious, inconsistent, rude, and impulsive, and still show love, joy, peace, patience, kindness, goodness, faithfulness, gentleness and self-control. In case you have forgotten, child, *your* job is to cultivate the fruit of the Spirit" (see Galatians 5:22-23).

This is one of the observations to be noted in the parable of the tares. Not until the good seed "sprang up and bore grain" did the weeds become evident (Matthew 13:26). God wants us to display the fruit of the Spirit to provide a marked contrast to the ways of the world. As difficult as it is to grow and flourish alongside a value system that threatens to choke out cherished Christian principles and values, we are to "grow together until the harvest" (Matthew 13:30). It will then be God's responsibility to judge, not ours. In the meantime we are told: "Do not be overcome by evil, but overcome evil with good" (Romans 12:21).

Light: "Blessed is the man who trusts in the Lord and whose trust is the Lord. For he will be like a tree planted by the water, that extends its roots by a stream and will not fear when the heat comes; but its leaves will be green, and it will not be anxious in a year of drought nor cease to yield fruit" (Jeremiah 17:7-8).

Reflection: Am I allowing God to cultivate the fruit of the Spirit in my life, or am I too busy trying to uproot the weeds of the world?

Too Taxing?

*Do not exasperate your children
that they may not lose heart.*
Colossians 3:21

We live in that buffer zone of civilization called a suburb. A big yard means higher taxes, and so we plant a garden to offset the added expense.

As we rake and hoe and water and sow, dozens of beady black eyes watch from every tree. Suburban birds have an insatiable appetite for fresh garden seeds. To discourage such feathered filchers I send my tomcat out to stand guard.

Should the neighbor see him ruffling the tail feathers of a robin, she lets her dog out to chase my cat. The dog promptly pollutes the ecology of my front yard, and I give chase with the broom.

Horrified, protective kids who think I am out to hasten the extinction of canines come stampeding through the garden to rescue their dog from the territory of the Mad Mopper. Indignant, friend hubby builds a fence to keep out the kids who are chasing the dogs who are after the cat who is after the birds who eat the seeds from the garden that is supposed to lower our tax. Ironically, the government considers the fence an improvement and raises our taxes.

Caught in such a vicious cycle of property development and tax assessment, disgruntled homeowners sometimes lose initiative. Penalized for making improvements, discouragement becomes a subtle form of self-destruction. Paint peels, porches sag, fences lean, value drops.

I believe there is a parallel here in the upkeep of the relationship we develop with our children. In our desire to protect them from the ravages of undesirable intruders who encroach upon the values we wish to see cultivated in their lives, we are inclined to enroll them in all sorts of positive programs involving sports and music and art and drama, with little or no forethought as to the final burden it creates.

Aggressive parents who pounce on every opportunity to improve their child's development, however, can also overtax him in a vicious circle of social and educational involvement. Pushed and pressured to achieve, perform, excel – physically, mentally, and emotionally – an exasperated child may react quite opposite to his parents' expectations. Interest wanes, effort lags, willpower weakens, and self-esteem drops.

Wise is the parent who can make a fair assessment of his child's capabilities, who can raise incentive yet not levy discouragement, who can explore potential without exploiting talent.

In that delicate balance that exists between parents and child, we have to remember that doing too much can sometimes be as destructive as doing nothing at all.

Light: "When I was a child, I used to speak as a child, think as a child, reason as a child; when I became a man, I did away with childish things" (1 Corinthains 13:11).

Reflection: Have I forgotten what it was like to be young? Am I overtaxing my child with expectations too deman-ding for his energy and emotions?

Valentine Day

For He knows the secrets of the heart.
Psalm 44:21

𝒫icture a great hulking football player charging down the aisle of a drugstore, the cans of hair spray tottering in his wake. Suddenly he digs in his cleats and makes a grab for a big red Valentine. Tucking it under his arm, he tiptoes sheepishly to the cashier.

Then imagine a dapper young man-about-town-type who swaggers into the lingerie section of the department store on February 14. All at once he turns into a stammering, red-faced idiot who can't remember his own name.

And picture a little boy with nose pressed flat against the glass of the candy counter. With utmost difficulty he manages to pass up the lollipops in favor of "a dollar's worth of peanut brittle, for my mommy, for Valentine's day. It's her very favorite!"

Or picture old Gramps tottering to the post office. As

he passes the general store he stops to size up the Valentines on display. Squinting through the bottom half of his bifocals, he chooses a card to his liking, pecks on the window with his cane to notify the clerk of his selection, and then hobbles in to pay for it. With fumbling hands he tucks the Valentine into the pocket of his tweed overcoat. Then all at once he squares his shoulders, hooks the cane over his left arm, and starts for home with sprightly step.

Oddly enough, such a miraculous transformation in a man's outlook is not due to some spontaneous burst of sentiment originating from his natural instincts, for men are annoyingly practical. It is, instead, the direct result of a subtle campaign by women in general – and his wife in particular – to educate him in the finer aspects of romance. Motivated by the desire to please, he responds to her expectations.

"There is," said wise old Solomon, "a time to love" (Ecclesiastes 3:8), a time to willingly, deliberately, ignore the more practical aspects of everyday living and make room for those small tokens of affection otherwise pushed into the far corner of our priorities.

For those who argue that among the more pressing problems of poverty, hunger, and disease such expressions of sentiment do not warrant a second thought, my only response is this: In a world filled with ugliness, corruption, and stench, did God really need a rose?

We are made in the image of our Creator, and yet

because we are caught up in the struggle to provide the basic necessities of life, we forget that a *balanced* approach is necessary to meet the needs of the individual. Our complex nature flourishes not only with physical provision but with emotional reinforcement, not only with mental stimulation but with spiritual fulfillment.

Light: "Delight yourself in the Lord, and He will give you the desires of your heart" (Psalm 37:4).

Reflection: Do I take the opportunities to cheer those who are deprived of the extras of life by surprising them with little tokens of love?

A Recycled Soul

For the Son of Man has come to seek
and to save that which was lost.
Luke 19:10

On cleaning day I resemble a mobile lost-and-found department. I have stray pins tucked into my hair, a lapel punctured by needles, a chain of safety pins swinging from my buttonhole. One pocket sags with nails, screws, and bolts, and the other bulges with pencils, pens, crayons, erasers, paper clips, nail files, thumbtacks, and rubber bands – plus all sorts of unidentified *lying* objects. They have been lying around so long I forget what they are!

But I must never dispose of them. Sooner or later someone will come along and say, "Did you see a thing that looks like such and such?" whereupon I go to the junk drawer and produce the item that most clearly matches the description. For one fleeting moment a little fellow's face beams with delight. He's actually got a mother who recognizes the value of a little rubber gasket from a water-powered rocket launcher when she sees one!

Or perhaps one of those clever people who are handy with crafts will phone to see if I have any "junk" saved for their latest project. Their ingenuity always amazes me, for they can take what others throw away – tin cans, plastic bottles, or styrofoam trays – and creatively transform them into attractive and useful items.

There was a time when I saw my very existence as just another questionable piece of junk, a scrap of humanity cluttering up the landscape of life, inevitably relegated to the garbage can of God's choosing. But from His word I realized that God looks upon us as redeemable, "not wishing for any to perish but for all to come to repentance" (2 Peter 3:9). He sent His Son to reclaim what would otherwise be lost.

Written in the Book of Life are the names of all sorts of souls whom other people may not value, but whom God could not bear to throw away because at some point in life they trusted Christ as Savior. When they did, He transformed their lives into attractive and useful witnesses for Him. "If any man is in Christ, he is a new creature; the old things passed away; behold, new things have come" (2 Corinthians 5:17).

With the passage of time, however, nagging doubts may arise as to the "keeping power" of God: *Am I still*

His child? Have I sinned too much to be forgiven? Will I still go to heaven when I die? The reassurance comes in verses such as John 6:37, where Jesus says, "All that the Father gives Me shall come to Me, and the one who comes to Me I will certainly not cast out." Yes, God is in the business of recycling lost souls: "And I am convinced that He is able to guard what I have entrusted to Him until that day" (2 Timothy 1:12).

Light: "'For I know the plans that I have for you,' declares the Lord, 'plans for welfare and not for calamity to give you a future and a hope. Then you will call upon Me and come and pray to Me, and I will listen to you. And you will seek Me and find Me, when you search for Me with all your heart. And I will be found by you,' declares the Lord" (Jeremiah 29:11-14).

Reflection: Is my new life in Christ evident to those I meet? Am I truly grateful for my transformed life?

Prejudice and Pride

Using both the right hand and the left to sling stones.
1 Chronicles 12:2

$\mathcal{J}$ am a mean, miserable, insensitive, oldfashioned mother.

I hate blue jeans.

I have hated them ever since I had to wear my brother's old denim overalls to clean out the chicken house. My pet hen eyed me with cool *cackle*-ation, head cocked sideways, haughty disdain emanating from her amber eye. She probably figured anyone wearing overalls carried a slingshot in his hind pocket, and such a cruel association put a definite strain on our relationship. It was months before I could regain her confidence.

I still have no use for blue jeans. When new they smell like raw linseed oil and are as flexible as awning canvas. When worn, they are as faded as dust rags and just as frayed. As I see it, there is no happy medium with blue

60

jeans. They make the fat look fatter and the thin look starved. They make the rich look ragged and the poor look wretched. They make the young look sloppy and the old look ancient. They cost a fortune and look worse than hand-me-downs.

I detest mending jeans because they offer such stout resistance to the sewing machine. Denim wears the point of the needle right down to the eye, then snaps it in two and spits it across the sewing room. The ordeal is so frustrating there have been times I could have torn the offending jeans from crotch to cuff and relished the thought of tossing them into the fire.

It is strange how prejudice provokes impatience toward clothes, customs, or people. Just because I was forced to wear my brother's old overalls to clean the chicken house, I associate denim with unpleasant tasks, dirty work, and peculiar odors. That my pet hen took exception to the overalls has no basis in fact. She may have been just as frightened had I worn any other kind of clothing. It was just easier to blame the loss of her confidence on the blue denim overalls, since I despised them anyway.

And since mending never has been one of my favorite chores, fixing holes in blue jeans is even less appealing under the circumstances. Rather than blaming my frustrations on my own impatience and inferior machine needles, it is easier to take out my resentment on the denim.

Such unpleasant memories of past experiences can

sometimes trigger off all sorts of unfair generalizations. Because one person from a different ethnic background offended us, we label them all. Because one was a traitor, we mistrust the rest. Because a few of them failed our expectations, we shoot holes in the reputation of all minority groups. And sitting smugly in the center of our prejudice, we can always find plenty of ammunition with which to load our arguments, even if it is nothing more than pebbles of trivial criticism propelled from our slingshots of pride.

Light: "In the way you judge, you will be judged; and by your standard of measure, it shall be measured to you" (Matthew 7:2).

Reflection: Am I making fair assessments of people based on individual cases and sound facts? Or is my personal prejudice influencing my attitudes and behavior?

Remember New Recruits

Who can stand before His cold?
Psalm 147:17

I have always considered November the coldest month of the year in central Canada. My blood is still thin from Indian summer, and my long underwear isn't unpacked from storage. So I suffer the grim consequences, gritting my teeth behind purple lips as the north wind spirals up my pant leg and out my sleeve.

Under normal conditions the tomcat does not react adversely to the climate, but when the November wind starts whistling under the door, it seems to activate the glue in the floor mat, and the tomcat sits there as if stuck to the premises. Periodically I peel him off and push him outside. He returns immediately, amusing himself indoors with such spectator sports as bird-watching. The frustration of seeing a hardy sparrow hop about just outside the window is sufficient to send spasmodic convulsions down his caudal appendage, but beyond that he refuses to budge.

I can't say I blame him. Except for unusual reasons, nobody leaves the snug warmth of hearth 'n' home to abandon himself to bleak November days. It is significant, therefore, that on November 11, hushed crowds gather at Canadian cenotaphs to pay tribute to those who served our country in time of war.

And so it should be. "If a man live many years, and rejoice in them all; yet let him remember the days of darkness" (Ecclesiastes 11:8, KJV).

Yes, Lord, help me to remember the veterans who served in the armed forces, but in terms of spiritual warfare, help me also to remember the cadets, the new believers who have but recently put on "the full armor of God" (Ephesians 6:11-17). Feeling warm and safe and relatively victorious in my current relationship with the Lord, I forget those initial battles against the enemy. The front line was not easily defined, and I often found myself in no-man's-land, a vulnerable target caught between opposing forces of good and evil. Desperately needing acceptance yet unable to distinguish friend from foe, at times I played traitor to both. Unable to gain spiritual victory in my Christian walk, the temptation was strong to succumb to despair. Had the Lord not "girded me with strength for battle" (Psalm 18:9), I may have abandoned the ranks of believers and surrendered to defeat.

As a veteran of the faith, therefore, I want to exercise patience and understanding for those awkward new recruits in the Lord's army. I need to venture out of my comfortable cocoon and take time to commend them for their stand, falling into rank beside them as they march out to face the foe. Together may we hoist our banner to the Prince of Peace.

Light: "'Not by might nor by power, but by My spirit,' says the Lord of hosts" (Zechariah 4:6).

Reflection: Am I doing something to specifically encourage a new Christian? Do I remember my own battles as a new believer so that I am not condescending about another's skirmishes with the enemy?

Hearing but Not Listening?

Wanting to have their ears tickled ... will
turn away their ears from the truth.
2 Timothy 4:3-4

*L*ast spring our teenage son decided it was time to upgrade his wheels. The first step was to try to sell his present vehicle. It was, shall we say, not exactly in mint condition. In fact, it wheezed and sputtered up the driveway and all but expired in a cloud of blue smoke.

Our son was on the verge of despair. "I'll *never* be able to sell that thing now!"

Friend hubby is the salesman in the family. "Just leave that to me."

A newspaper ad brought in a deluge of phone calls – the price bracket must have appealed to teenagers. After answering a number of inquiries, it dawned on me that

66

these young guys weren't interested in bying a car. They just wanted a radio on wheels. When they found out there was a jalopy available that had a radio, a cassette deck, and four speakers, I almost had to stand in the driveway calling, "Next number please," while friend hubby directed the traffic.

The first fellow to turn the radio on full blast wanted to buy the car. Friend hubby asked if he wanted to take it for a test run first.

"Yeah, maybe I should."

We could hear the radio blaring all around the block.

"I'll take it!" he shouted as he lurched to a stop and held out his money. Friend hubby valiantly tried to point out the things that needed immediate attention.

"Yeah, I guess so, but it can't be in too bad a shape. I couldn't hear nothin'."

To his way of thinking, "little things" like connecting rods, wrist pins, noisy tappets, piston slap, and a growling transmission were all secondary to the roar of a rock station.

As he drove away, I had the distinct feeling that there went a young man who still had a lesson to learn. What he didn't *want* to hear would one day leave him stranded.

This truth also has its spiritual parallel, pointed out by the apostle Paul as he attempted to impress upon young Timothy the importance of sound doctrine. Paul predicted that the time would come when people would refuse to accept biblical teaching, preferring instead to "turn aside to fruitless discussion" that was more in accordance with their own human desires (1 Timothy 1:6). As a devout Christian, however, Paul could testify that it was not some strange, outlandish tales that had kept him on the narrow road that leads to life eternal, but the power of Jesus, who said, "I am the way, the truth and the life: no man cometh unto the Father, but by me" (John 14:6, KJV). And while others who listened to false teachings fell by the wayside, Paul, who heeded the Word of God even while negotiating all the twists and turns of life, could say with firm conviction, "I have finished the course, I have kept the faith" (2 Timothy 4:7). No breakdowns along the way for him!

Light: "He whose ear listens to the life-giving reproof will dwell among the wise" (Proverbs 15:31).

Reflection: Above the noise and commotion of daily living, may I still be able to hear Your still, small voice, Lord.

Tricky Trails

*If I should say, "My foot has slipped," thy
lovingkindness, O Lord, will hold me up.*
Psalm 94:18

Long before cross-country skiing became the winter
equivalent to summer jogging, some of us decided it
was easier to go over snowbanks than to shovel our way
through them.

I have since realized just how progressive we were –
except for the fact that we didn't spend nearly enough
for our equipment. My first pair of skis were two boards
that my brother bent upwards by steaming them for hours
in the copper boiler on top of the kitchen stove. A few
leather straps from an old horse harness secured them
to my winter boots, and I was off! If the going got a bit
slow, waxing the skis with some floor wax and buffing
them with a piece of fleece-lined underwear speeded
things up.

Nobody ever told me that I was to stay strictly on level ground, so when I got the chance I took to the hills – in a big way. We lived two miles from a ski resort, and I'd whiz past the city slickers with their fancy equipment and never think twice about breaking a leg. My only concern was getting up the hill again. I must have weighed all of seventy pounds, and the tow rope kept lifting me up off my feet and tossing me off to the side.

I will be forever indebted to the old hometown Samaritan who always seemed to be around to rescue skiers in distress. When I was tangled up like a plate of spaghetti, what a glorious sight to see old Abner riding down the hill on his scoop shovel and swinging to a magnificent stop right at my side! A few brisk instructions and I would be back on my feet and speeding down the hills again like a pro.

The trip home seemed dismally slow by comparison, except for those spooky times when the coyotes started to howl as I entered the bush trail at twilight. I guarantee that no cross-country skier before or since has ever made better time, no matter how well equipped!

Perhaps the psalmist felt that same sense of urgency when he prayed, "Lead me in a level path, because of my foes" (Psalm 27:S11). Most of us have experienced the thrills and spills that are part of the Christian walk. We glow with exhilaration remembering the mountains we have conquered, or feel embarrassed recalling the many times we have fallen. We may even reminisce about the Good Samaritans who have picked us up and set us back on our spiritual feet.

But the memories that stand out stark against my mental landscape are those fears that nearly overwhelmed my progress as I ventured into the dark unknown, the enemy close upon my heels. If ever I felt threatened, inadequate, and alone, I prayed for nothing more than a level path and a speedy deliverance. In retrospect, however, I can testify to the unfailing goodness of God, who saw me safely through those twilight trails and whose presence was as warm and real as the old coal oil lamp that used to shine in the window of our farmhouse, beckoning me home after a long day of skiing.

Light: "My help comes from the Lord, who made heaven and earth. He will not allow your foot to slip; He who keeps you will not slumber" (Psalm 121:2-3).

Reflection: Lord, thank You that You hold me up wherever I go.

A Thankless Effort

All of us growl like bears, and moan sadly like doves; we hope for justice, but there is none.
Isaiah 59:11

In Canada teachers have a way of getting even with mothers: they announce a Junior Art and Science Fair every spring.

I can picture them gleefully assembled in the staff room, trying to decide upon the most inconvenient date possible. It must not be in early March, because there is still sufficient snow for the pupils to haul their projects to school on sleds. No, no, it *must* be sometime in April, when the roads are too wet for little red wagons and the wind is strong enough to ruin all but the most rigidly built projects. That's the time to have an Art and Science Fair – during April rains and spring break, when mothers are already at the cracking point trying to cope simultaneously with wet feet, runny noses, and muddy floors.

72

That's the time to remind them that they are lagging behind on artistic and cultural pursuits, the time to get them involved in the advancements of technology. Announce an Art and Science Fair. The kids will take it from there.

The first week they'll moan and groan and whine because they don't know what to make. Everything Mother suggests has already been done before – the balloon powered jet, the vinegar and soda volcano, the salt dough relief map of North America, the eggshell mosaic. They need something *new*. And so it's "Mom, can you take us to the library?" "Mom, can you find the stuff we need for this project?" "Mom, can you read us the directions?" "Mom ... Mom ... ?"

The second week they decide they're tired of their idea. Besides, it doesn't work right anyway. They want something different. "Mom, can we try ...?"

The third week it's "Mom, can you ... ?"

Just about the time mothers are drained of ideas and fatigued from refereeing the squabbles, the teachers send home a note: "This is to remind you [how could we forget?] of the upcoming Art and Science Fair to be held tomorrow and Friday. The students have put forth a great deal of time and effort [is that so?] in preparing their various projects, and we urge you, as parents, to attend. After viewing the displays we are sure you will want to commend each and every one for the initiative shown."

Although we grumble and complain about coping with

perceived injustices in life, no acknowledgment for our efforts really adds insult to injury! The typical reaction is to point out, not too tactfully at that, the contributions we have made toward the successful completion of some project of other. In response we may get the recognition we feel we *deserve*, but it is not the spontaneous appreciation we had *expected*.

Another alternative is to blow our own horn, yet Proverbs 27:2 says, "Let another praise you, and not your own mouth. Boasting of our own accomplishments is incompatible with Christian humility. Waiting in faith for God's commendation is not, however, and we can be certain He will acknowledge our efforts in His good time, despite feelings of being overlooked at the moment.

Light: "Lovingkindness is Thine, O Lord, for Thou dost recompense a man according to his work" (Psalm 62:12).

Reflection: Father, give me a true spirit of servanthood.

Steady Lights Needed

Let your light shine before men in such
a way that they may see your good works,
and glorify your Father who is in heaven.
Matthew 5:16

*E*ven with all the advancements in technology, nobody has yet invented a robot that wears an apron and holds a light at just the right angle to satisfy a do-it-yourself husband.

Over the years I must have stood by with my trusty light through hundreds of home repairs, emergency and otherwise. I once grew impatient and asked friend hubby if he knew that the hook on the trouble light was there for a purpose.

He grinned sheepishly. "Yeah, but if I just hang it up, it doesn't talk to me while I work."

And so I have been a combination light fixture and morale booster in all sorts of cramped quarters – reaching

75

up into the dark corners of the basement installing furnace ducts, hunched in the corner of the attic spreading insulation, dangling over a car fender in the dark doodling with a faulty ignition. My light has pointed the way down miles of pencil marks on paneling and across hundred of boards while friend hubby labored away, see-saw, see-saw, and I blew dust out of his path and into my shoes. The circular saw is faster, but instead of slivers in my socks it throws splinters in my eyes, and I can't see where to hold my light.

It's a tedious calling. When friend hubby suddenly appears with his red tool box, I don't exactly beam with pleasure at the prospect. After holding the light for what seems an eternity, my arms ache, my back gets a kink, and my arches cramp. And all the while I am haunted by the thought that I'm not achieving a solitary thing.

In moments like those I console myself with the thought that heaven is a perfect place, with no repair jobs and perfect lighting. Otherwise some immortal handyman might usher me in, hand me a candle, and I would still be holding the light a thousand years later while he fiddles with the latches of the pearly gates.

Some jobs just seem to take *that* long!

I should not be so impatient. Even letting "your light shine before men" implies more than a flash-in-the-pan type of Christian witness, more than one brilliant testimony or one dazzling display of good works. It indicates the steady glow of a consistent Christian walk, dependable qualities, sound character, and clear direction.

Whether reaching into the far corners of the world, standing by the sickbeds of the suffering, or dangling by the thin cord of hope in a doubtful situation, Christians hold out the only Light there is for people who are groping in spiritual darkness. We may not feel we are achieving much at the time, and our calling may be tedious, but the spiritual impact of our combined efforts cannot be measured this side of heaven.

Some jobs just take *that* long!

Light: "Thou dost light my lamp; the Lord my God illumines my darkness" (Psalm 18:28).

Reflection: May my life be a clear, shining testimony of Your grace.

Brooding Over
Glass Marbles?

They were disappointed for they had trusted,
they came there and were confounded.
Job 6:20

On a bleak November day a pair of pigeons landed on
the balcony of my sister's apartment. After looking
around, they decided that roosting on a carpeted balcony
three stories above the smog was superior to their
previous accommodations under bridge girders. Dining
at a bird-seed buffet had distinct advantages, especially
with winter approaching. Bill and Coo decided to stay,
much to my sister's amusement.

By December my sister felt the pigeons needed the
protection from the northwest wind that whistled around
the balcony, so she rigged up a cardboard box with a
forty-watt light bulb in it. Ah, here was gracious living

at its best! The penthouse apartment that every pair of pigeons dreams about!

With conditions so conducive to raising a family, Bill and Coo soon started plucking straws from the balcony broom and stockpiling them inside the box. Not long thereafter, in the middle of January, two premature pigeon eggs put in their appearance, and Bill started walking the balcony floor in anticipation of the blessed event.

Certain that fledglings could never survive in severe sub-zero temperatures, my sister secretly removed the pigeon eggs and replaced them with big glass marbles. Not the least bit wise, Mama pigeon finished out the incubation period as diligently as if she had been sitting on her own eggs. When nothing materialized, her complaints were both sad and touching – sad because she did not recognize the uselessness of her pursuit, touching because of her profound dedication.

Are you sitting on glass marbles by vainly nurturing false hope? Faith is an admirable quality, but only if the focus of our faith is based on actual potential. And yet the world is full of stories about people brooding over impossible endeavors. We chuckle about the illiterate dreamer who believes he is dictating a best seller, the monotone composer who is working on a sensational new opera, the plain Jane who has bought a one-way ticket to Hollywood. Such stories are sad but touching, because no matter how long they sit on them, the cold glass marbles of false hope will never hatch.

And yet all of us are more or less vulnerable. Like the deceived pigeon, we can spend considerable time and effort on a project or person only to meet with inevitable disappointment. Blind to anything but our own desires and motivated by strong instincts, we fail to distinguish reality from wishful thinking. As the writer of Ecclesiastes wisely observed, "In many dreams and in many words there is emptiness. Rather, fear God" (Ecclesiastes 5:7).

Light: "Trust in the Lord with all your heart, and do not lean on your own understanding. In all your ways acknowledge Him, and He will make your paths straight" (Proverbs 3:5-6).

Reflection: Help me to honestly evaluate my goals and pursue those that have the most potential in the light of eternity.

Triggering the Alarm

For the Lord your God is a consuming fire.
Deuteronomy 4:24

Fiend hubby was testing a newly installed smoke detector the other night, and it proved to be very effective. The tomcat went skidding down the hallway to the nearest exit, and the kids came running from the far corner of the basement to investigate the high-pitched squeal. They stood with their hands over their ears as he tried to explain what it was all about.

If the house ever *does* catch fire, there will be no use trying to give directions over the sound of that smoke detector. The only consolation lies in the fact that any normal human being will instinctively run in the opposite direction to preserve his eardrums.

Even that option did not exist in the days of my childhood, yet fire hazards in old farmhouses were as common as the stoves that heated them. It makes me wonder why smoke detectors weren't invented when they were sorely needed. Perhaps it is just as well. Grandpa, already frustrated in his attempts to light the old kitchen stove, would no doubt have hurled a stick of green wood right through the first smoke detector that betrayed his ineptitude. And anyone inadvertently closing the wrong damper on the stove pipe did not need the added stress of a smoke detector hurling insults. He was already the object of enough screaming tirades directed at him from other members of the family as they groped their way to the nearest door, madly flailing their arms in a cloud of blue smoke.

While we no longer have to cope with the idiosyncrasies of a blazing inferno tended on an hourly basis, neither are we as conscious of the dangers of fire. Lulled into smug complacency by our modern heating arrangements, and dependent upon a gadget that can alert us to the slightest operational flaw through the use of a smoke sensor, we have nearly ceased to recognize the latent power of flames. Yet unleashed from a furnace they can – and do – destroy us.

We are like the children of Israel. When Moses went up Mount Sinai to receive the Ten Commandments, "its smoke ascended like the smoke of a furnace," so that all the people who were in the camp trembled (Exodus 19:18). Observing the mighty power of God firsthand instilled fear and respect, but gradually the memory faded. By the time the children of Israel reached the relative ease of the Promised Land, God had to warn them of His latent potential. "Watch yourself ... otherwise the anger of the Lord your God will be kindled against you" (Deuteronomy 6:12-15).

Although restrained by His love for mankind, the wrath of God's anger and His fiery judgments burn hotly against evil. Lulled into materialistic complacency, the world no longer recognizes the awesome power that can – and does – destroy the wicked. We as Christians must therefore act as smoke detectors, warning others of the perils of spiritual negligence.

Light: "Sound an alarm on My holy mountain! Let all the inhabitants of the land tremble, for the day of the Lord is coming; surely it is near" (Joel 2:1).

Reflection: The fire that warms the hearts of believers will also destroy the souls of unrepentant sinners unless I point them to the way of escape through faith in Jesus Christ.

On Guard

Deliver my soul from the sword, my
only life from the power of the dog.
Psalm 22:20

To say Max the dog is big is the understatement of the year. I have watched him out of the corner of my eye ever since he took up residence in the neighborhood. In summer he sits on his owner's front porch, his long Roman nose just clearing the railing. Eyes alert, ears cocked, enormous tongue salivating – he is an ominous canine threat if ever there was one. In winter Max takes up guard duty behind the picture window, no doubt drooling on the coffee table whenever meaty-looking legs walk by.

He's even bigger up close than he is from the road, an overpowering chief-of-police dog with fangs to match. When I had to call on the lady of the house, it was a definite reassurance to notice she kept a firm grip on his collar while I timidly reached out my hand to pet him. One gulp and my arm would have disappeared to the elbow.

The fact that Max stays on his yard and I stay on mine is a foregone conclusion. One could say it is a safe arrangement, but it's not too satisfying. I can think of any number of bones I could offer to him if only he were the more approachable sort. And Max probably imagines what a good meal *I* would make if only the dog catcher didn't annihilate big pooches who devour little old ladies. So here we sit, our perceived need for mutual self-preservation preventing us from enjoying one another.

The irony of the whole situation is that even if Max were no bigger than a toy poodle, I would still be afraid of him, because I have no experience with guard dogs. But coop me up with the biggest, fiercest cat imaginable, and I am a regular Daniel in the lions' den.

Such is the inconsistency of our fears based on the unknown. Ten of the Israelites who went to spy on Canaan were so intimidated they reported, "All the people whom we saw in it are men of great size ... and we became like grasshoppers in our own sight, and so we were in their sight" (Numbers 13:32-33). Yet Caleb and Joshua received no such impression, the difference being that their faith in God's protection superseded any fears that the impending confrontation spawned.

While unfamiliarity may multiply anxieties when we

are young, old age also has a way of distorting our perception and multiplying our insecurities. As an inexperienced youth, David killed the giant Goliath with a slingshot. But as a seasoned warrior, David felt helpless against ordinary foes, whom he described as raging bulls, roaring lions, and savage dogs, threatening him on every side (Psalm 22).

Whether warranted or irrational, fear is common to us all, and our reactions are much the same. We withdraw into the perceived safety of our own little world, there to view with suspicion anything that even remotely threatens us. Yet, instead of retreating from reality, we can call upon God as our one source of help in all situations.

Light: "God is our refuge and strength, a very present help in trouble" (Psalm 46:1).

Reflection: Lord, help me to focus less on my own fears and more on the courage You can give.

In the Economy of God

Not slothful in business; fervent in spirit; serving the Lord.
Romans 12:11, KJV

It was not the usual ho-hum drawn-out game of Monopoly®. In fact, just making correct change provoked lively and heated debates, but they kept at it – two ten-year-old boys tackling real-life issues such as taxes and rent and whether or not to invest in Utilities or Park Place. Once in a while the banker would be admonished for not handing over the proper wages when somebody passed Pay Day. When you're young and impatient, promptness commands a great deal of respect. Tardiness gets what it deserves – a good loud chewing out, no holds barred!

Things would quiet down as the young businessmen shrewdly assessed their piles of money and real estate. Now and then they paused to negotiate a deal. If things were going too slowly, they agreed, amicably, to change the rules for the benefit of all concerned.

The seriousness of the game was interrupted at one point when the tomcat, hitherto a silent partner, suddenly lunged at the game and sent the assets flying in all directions. Such an intrusion was tolerable, indeed amusing, but when he turned around and decided to monopolize the entire business by lying down in the middle of the board, that was too much. Out came bribes in the form of milk and cat food.

The tomcat having been lured away, it was back to the board and on with the game. Ten minutes. Fifteen minutes. I had to admire these boys. They were really staying with it.

I was therefore surprised when five minutes later the game was suddenly over. "Why, what's the matter?" I asked. "Did you get all mixed up?"

"Naw," replied the one fellow, casting a withering glance at his opponent. "He's just sore cuz he's poor, so I'm quittin'!" And with that he strode out of the room.

Sometimes we too reach the point where we no longer want to play the game of finances, nor does anybody want to play it with us. Pay day is neither sure nor rewarding. Our capital is limited, our real estate unprofitable. Perhaps a silent partner has pounced on our assets, or we have had to buy him out, creating an unexpected setback. After long months of intensive struggle, our reaction to losing is often predictable: "We're sore cuz we're poor."

Rather than throwing up our hands and quitting, there is a possibility of benefiting from such experience. The writer of Proverbs notes that "to the hungry soul every bitter thing is sweet" (Proverbs 27:7, KJV). If we are hungry enough to succeed, we will write off a financial loss as a valuable learning experience and try again. If we have taken prosperity for granted in the past, we will certainly be more grateful in the future. If we have valued the wrong priorities, God can use our loss for His gain.

The world has no monopoly on good sports. Christians with right attitudes are winners even when they lose.

Light: "Better is a little with the fear of the Lord, than great treasure and turmoil with it" (Proverbs 15:16).

Reflection: Father, help me to adjust my value system so as to have a godly perspective in all areas of life.

Spurred on to Repentance

*I returned and saw under the sun, that the race is not
to the swift, nor the battle to the strong ... nor yet favour
to men of skill; but time and chance happeneth to them all.*
Ecclesiastes 9:11, KJV

A newspaper article summing up the work involved
in organizing a rodeo concluded by saying, "Rodeos
don't just happen."

I don't know about that! As I recall, some pretty good
entertainment was provided spontaneously on the farm.
When I was growing up, it wasn't a cowboy who wore
the spurs but a big white rooster. When he ruffled his
neck feathers and flashed his amber eye, smart people
headed for the nearest door.

We were playing ball one day, and in the heat of
competition I failed to notice the approach of my arch
enemy. Panic welled up within me, and I let fly with the
baseball bat. The rooster keeled over, and we gathered

90

around his body, deciding what ought to be done. I concluded there was but one course of action: I would have to confess my "fowl" deed.

Trembling, I approached the back step, only to hear my mother sharpening the butcher knife. She had observed the whole episode from the kitchen window and decided that now was as good a time as any for a pot of rooster noodle soup. Much relieved, I went out to gather up the main ingredient.

That rooster was tougher than we thought. He had not only survived the "fatal" blow, but was back on his feet and ready for the next event! Right until the day he laid his spurs to rest, I had to be wary of him lurking around the corners.

The dread of that old rooster became so indelibly etched on my mind that I see him yet whenever I read the story of Peter's denial. Like me, Peter was bold until confronted off guard. Too frightened to run, too weak to stand, he impulsively lashed out in a vain attempt to defend himself. "And immediately a cock crowed" (Matthew 26:74). To my way of thinking, it was not any old cock, but a big white rooster with ruffled neck feathers and sharp spurs, flashing its accusing eye! I can identify with Peter's plight.

We never *intend* to deny Christ, anymore than I intended to kill the rooster, but in unguarded moments, "time and chance happeneth to [us] all." Threatened by an unexpected confrontation, we Christians have moments when we are too frightened to run and too weak to stand, so we instinctively resort to the basic, human reaction of lashing out at the object of our fears. And then the awful realization that we have killed our testimony fills us with remorse.

Like an understanding mother who forgives our impulsive moves, however, Christ stands ready to redeem the good from the bad, so long as we come to Him in confession for our foul deeds.

Light: "No temptation has overtaken you but such as is common to man; and God is faithful, who will not allow you to be tempted beyond what you are able, but with the temptation will provide the way of escape also, that you may be able to endure it" (1 Corinthians 10:13).

Reflection: Father, I praise You that upon confession of my sins, You erase my guilt and give me a fresh start.

A Proper Diet

*Always learning and never able to
come to the knowledge of the truth.*
2 Timothy 3:7

A modern expert in child care claims that a chubby baby with dimples in his knees should be viewed as a distressing sight because fat babies grow up to be obese adults plagued by heart attacks, hypertension, and diabetes. He goes on to try to persuade young mothers that a baby who has been fed within the last three hours is *not* hungry. He may be crying at the top of his lungs, but Mother should rest assured that he is *not* hungry. Starving to death, perhaps, or fevered from dehydration, but *not* hungry – of that the expert is absolutely certain. Does he not have a tidy little bit of research in black and white to prove it?

I am skeptical.

This same expert also says that a toddler should be

93

allowed to eat only what he *wants* to eat. I have reservations about that kind of "expert" advice, mainly because I question the food value of stones, potting soil, marbles, and the contents of the cat's dish. Yet every mother knows that these are favorite snacks of toddlers.

But we *misunderstand*, claims the expert. Children are not to be *exposed* to snacks. A child who is not offered cookies and candies early in life will not develop a craving for sweets.

Has he not realized that every child is born with a nose that can sniff out a cookie jar faster than a bloodhound? Or pick up the trail of a half-eaten gumdrop even after it has rolled clear down the hall and disappeared beneath the bed in a cloud of dust?

Somehow the advice of such experts always pales in the light of reality. For instance, there are thousands of believers who made genuine commitments to Christ at an early age, and yet "experts" question their claims, insisting children are incapable of making such lasting spiritual decisions. Consequently, some young parents are not only discouraged from bringing up a child "in the discipline and instruction of the Lord" (Ephesians 6:4), they are advised to raise a child on spiritually neutral ground so that he can choose his beliefs for himself.

What such people tragically overlook is that a child allowed to spiritually ingest whatever he pleases tends to gravitate toward stones, potting soil, and marbles, because the broad road that leads to destruction is the inevitable choice of sinful human nature.

And yet at the same time, every child seems to be born with an instinctive thirst for God. He may be crying out for direction in life, starving for lack of purpose, or feverishly trying to fill the void in his life, yet he is never satisfied. It is therefore our responsibility as parents to introduce him at every opportunity to the "pure milk of the word, that by it [he] may grow in respect to salvation" (1 Peter 2:2).

Light: "Blessed are those who hunger and thirst for righteousness, for they shall be satisfied" (Matthew 5:6).

Reflection: Am I instilling in my children Christian truths and godly principles, both by word and in deed?

At That Vulnerable Age

All things are lawful, but not all things are profitable.
1 Corinthians 10:23

The neighbors have a little fellow a year old who is making his mother age before her time. When she lets him out he eats everything in sight – stone, grass, sticks, sand, and dandelions. This week he developed a taste for petunias. He snapped off a prize bloom and poked it down the hatch quick as a wink.

"And to think I sterilized everything he used just a few months ago!" his mother moaned in despair. Junior, meanwhile, is doing just fine, flashing a mischievous grin with two rabbit teeth top and bottom.

She brought him over for a visit the other day. I quickly learned that our house is no longer toddler proof. In no time he had found a safety pin, a marble, a delicious plant, half a dozen books that looked good enough to eat, and a tomcat that looked like a stuffed toy. Chomp!

He even wound this one up by biting its tail. The reaction was immediate and painful.

I have a deep and abiding sympathy for mothers with youngsters of that age. It is, however, neither deep enough nor sufficiently abiding to warrant my services as a baby-sitter. Toddlers are not babies, and they *rarely* sit. In fact, I have still not recuperated from the time our own children were that age, and the oldest is already married.

I guess I would say I am too old to be a young mother and too young to be an old grandmother. Like the neighbor's toddler, I am right in one of those transition stages of life. I am delightfully free from the confining restraints of responsibilities but woefully vulnerable to wrong choices.

What I had hitherto only been able to observe from the sidelines now invites my total involvement because of increased mobility. What had previously been passive enjoyment now tempts my active participation because of easier access. What had formerly been just an occasional taste of pleasure now whets my appetite because of the freedom to choose. Will I gobble up everything in sight without exercising descretion and foresight?

Middle-aged people in my position can wander in all sorts of directions in search of amusements, but in the light of eternity, are the rewards of some of these endeavors not much more than "wood, hay, [and] straw?"

(1 Corinthians 3:12). While I can identify with those who have extra time on their hands, I believe as a Christian that my days are neither long enough nor of sufficient duration to warrant their waste on excessive temporal pleasures. I believe Scripture exhorts me instead to invest my time and resources into becoming a more mature, productive Christian.

Light: "Godliness is profitable for all things, since it holds promise for the present life and also for the life to come" (1 Timothy 4:8).

Reflection: Lord, guide me as I seek to discover all You have in store for me to do, and thank You for the ability to do them.

The Acid Test

And I will multiply the fruit of the
tree and the produce of the field.
Ezekiel 36:30

In view of the abundant gardens God has provided for us over the years, I have never had patience to make things in small amounts. Why make three quarts of pickles when it's just as simple to make thirty? Why preserve only a peck of tomatoes when there is a bushel to be done? Why make two ittybitty jars of jelly when the crab apple trees are loaded? Why indeed?

Because jelly-making equipment is not available in Paul Bunyan capacities, that's why. When I decided to make a *real* batch of jelly, I discovered I was on my own.

Fine and dandy. First I washed as many apples as my double sinks would hold, and then I transferred the whole works into the biggest blue enamel kettle I could find in

Grandma's basement.

As I stood over the simmering caldron, slowly stirring the contents with a wooden spoon, I tried to decide the most efficient way of straining the juice. I knew I was going to be dealing with a lot of pulp – a little twobit jelly bag was out of the question – so I wiped the steam from my bifocals and put on my thinking cap.

Peering down into the unfinished basement, I spied a sturdy spike protruding from a floor joist. Aha! Just the thing on which to hang an oversized jelly bag. But where to find one? Among the old pillowcases, of course!

I emptied my kettle of apple pulp into an old pillow slip, hung it on the spike, and put the dishpan on the floor underneath to catch the drips.

The next morning I went downstairs and found the dishpan nearly full of juice. I could now dispose of the pulp by spreading it on the garden, which was in dire need of organic enrichment anyway.

Unfortunately, I overlooked two important factors: crab apples are high in acid and old pillowcases are low in resistance. I was struggling up the basement stairs with my heavy sack of apple pulp when – plop! The pillowcase burst open. There was apple pulp splattered on the wall, apple pulp creeping down the stairs, apple pulp oozing from the torn sack like lava creeping from a sluggish volcano, and there I stood, Mrs. Paul Bunyan herself, trapped ankle deep in apple pulp and feeling about two inches tall.

In retrospect, I certainly can appreciate the wisdom of letting "your moderation be known.unto all men" (Philippians 4:5, KJV). We are surrounded by an abundance of good things on every side, and it is difficult to be content with small amounts of money, or food, or clothes, or entertainment. Does availability not justify excess?

But *more* is not always *better*. We forget that indulgence is high in temptation, and we are low in resistance. In our constant striving up the ladder of success, our weak moral fiber is apt to tear open under the load, leaving us trapped in the insidious pulp of materialism.

Light: "The Lord makes poor and rich; He brings low, He also exalts" (1 Samuel 2:7).

Reflection: "Give me neither poverty nor riches; feed me with the food that is my portion" (Proverbs 30:8).

The Problems of
Interior Decorating

May peace be within your walls.
Psalm 122:7

When someone says she has been hanging wallpaper, I know what she means. But like so many other terms, "hanging wallpaper" does not convey the whole truth of the matter. The ideal, perhaps, but not the reality. Wallpaper does not *hang*. It sags, pulls, twists, tears, slips, sticks, and wrinkles, but it does *not* hang, except under rare and unusual circumstances. Anything that hangs must of necessity be passive and supple and easily manipulated.

Wallpaper is nothing of the sort.

I can coax it and plead with it and pray over it, but wallpaper retains a mind of its own, resisting like a stubborn mule my persistent efforts to tug and pull it hither and yon. Let a professional paperhanger come on the scene, however, and the wallpaper turns to putty in his hands. But then wallpaper always has had a distorted sense of humor.

For example, the wallpaper in the book that boldly promised to be such a perfect complement to the rest of my decor often makes quite the opposite statement once it is hung, becoming nothing more than a dull, lifeless resemblance of its former self. Yet the pattern that looked absolutely dead on the showroom shelf may suddenly spring to life, jumping out at me from the wall at home and overpowering the entire room with one shrill scream of color and design.

And yet for all its faults, wallpaper has its redeeming qualities. I have papered rooms in crooked old houses where despair set in before I'd even unrolled my tape measure. Lo and behold if the wallpaper didn't obligingly cover a multitude of sins. But I can never count on it. Given a nice straight room, the pattern is just as apt to go askew.

Every time I redecorate, therefore, the thought occurs to me that hanging wallpaper is like surrendering willpower. The term only conveys the ideal, not the reality. The truth of the matter is that anyone who surrenders his will must of necessity be submissive, obedient, and humble in spirit – and most of us are nothing of the sort. We are rebellious, wayward, and proud – and we do not appreciate being "pasted to the wall" and shown where we belong.

Surrender of the will means a matching of the wits. From the spiritual perspective, it is the cutting down of self in order to measure up to God's standards. Refusal to do so is to defy self-improvement. We can be coaxed and pleaded with and prayed over but we may still insist upon having our own way. Yet a few deft turns in the hands of the right Person, and we can become amazingly compliant. For while willpower has the inclination to resist, it also has potential to submit.

Surrender to God in each new situation, therefore, usually means a time of inner turmoil and confusion while we seek to apply His principles to our lives, as we do our spiritual "wallpapering." As we yield, however, the result is a fresh new perspective on a jaded outlook, and peace within our walls.

Light: "For the Lord taketh pleasure in his people: he will beautify the meek with salvation" (Psalm 149:4).

Reflection: Father, help me to give priority to my internal adorning, the "imperishable quality of a gentle and quiet spirit, which is precious in the sight of God" (1 Peter 3:3-4).

Not My Cup of Tea

*See to it that no one takes you captive through philosophy
and empty deception, according to the tradition of men,
according to the elementary principles of the world.*
Colossians 2:8

𝕴n this part of the country, any organization that considers itself the least bit cultured seems bound by tradition to observe an annual ritual known as the "spring tea," and the rest of us are usually issued an invitation. Whether or not this is an overt attempt to educate us in the finer things of life, or just a subtle way of soliciting money for depleted coffers, I can't really say, but I know spring has arrived when invitations to tea flood both the media and the mailbox.

Quite frankly, I have never acquired a taste for tea, even in the company of good friends, much less amid the stiff formality of aloof strangers. In my estimation, steeping it in a silver pot and sipping it from dainty china cups still does nothing whatsoever to enhance the flavor.

On those rare occasions when I have dared to voice my opinion, I have been given to understand that "one does not go to a spring tea because one likes tea." I take it one goes to prove one is not a social clod.

From my observation, one also goes to show off one's new spring hat, or because one aspires to the honor of pouring tea, or because one has been taken socially captive by a cultured matron who is convinced that a spring tea is the epitome of all social graces combined, and one declines her invitation at one's peril.

There are, you see, those who are convinced that the eventual demise of the annual spring tea will indicate the end of civilization as we know it.

I can hardly wait.

In my estimation, rituals rooted in tradition and propagated through peer pressure have nothing worthwhile to offer anyway.

This was the essence of Paul's argument to those early believers who were inclined to submit themselves to outdated religious observances. Dietary restrictions, ceremonial rites, festival obligations, and sabbath laws had been initially instituted by God as symbolic *shadows* of that which was to come (Colossians 2:16). Over the years, however, the observance of such rituals became a substitute for personal faith. The *doing* became more important than the *believing* – the shadow became the substance of worship.

Deluded by persuasive arguments and peer pressure, we too can be in danger of substituting philosophy for faith, tradition for truth, and rituals for righteousness, all "in accordance with the commandments and teachings of men" (Colossians 2:22; italics added). Jesus, however, reminded the Samaritan woman that "God is spirit, and those who worship Him must worship" Him – not in ceremony and tradition – but "in spirit and truth" (John 4:24).

Light: "Know that ye were not redeemed ... from your vain conversation received by tradition from your fathers; but with the precious blood of Christ" (1 Peter 1:18, KJV).

Reflection: Am I depending upon the observance of meaningless rituals for salvation, or do I believe that the one supreme sacrifice Christ made on the cross is sufficient for me?

On the Horns
of a Dilemma

*Be not far from me, for trouble is near; for there
is none to help. Many bulls have surrounded
me; strong bulls ... have encircled me.*
Psalm 22:11-12

𝓕riend hubby was only a lad in knickers the last time he
set foot on the old Barkman homestead in Kansas, but
he vaguely recalled wading in a creek that ran through
the pasture, and he was anxious to see it again. Assured
by his elderly cousin that Cottonwood Creek was indeed
still trickling along, friend hubby took off ahead of me
at a brisk pace, leaving me to pick and choose my own
way through the thorns and nettles and barbed wire
fences.

Finding myself in the middle of a Kansas cow pasture
wearing open-toed sandals, I was, shall we say, walking

rather circumspectly. When at last I chanced to look up, I realized with horror that I was in the very same meadow as the biggest, blackest bull I had ever seen.

It wasn't that he was so close to me – yet. It was just that friend hubby seemed so far away.

I tried yelling, but to no avail. Cottonwood Creek had far more attraction for friend hubby than some old black bull who was merely threatening his wife. I thought of running, but decided instead to walk very, very fast. I didn't want to give that bull the idea that I was afraid of him, or anything like that. And besides, he was acting very respectably, just standing there in the far, far corner of the pasture, staring at me.

I hurried on, not even daring to look back, but even as I bent down to crawl through the barbed wire fence to safety, I fully expected to feel a sharp pair of horns giving me one last powerful assist.

Cautiously I straightened up and looked around.

The bull hadn't moved.

When I caught up to friend hubby, he explained why he had been so indifferent to my plight. The big, black bull was a gentle, young Angus *cow*.

Trying to pick and choose our way circumspectly through the thorns and nettles and barbed wire fences that life imposes, we sometimes feel that God has left us far behind, that He is oblivious to the dangers confronting us, indifferent to our pleas. Even so valiant a warrior as King David fearfully imagined enemy soldiers to be like raging bulls with lowered horns, charging at him from every side.

I know the feeling.

I also remember the great sense of relief when friend hubby, with greater knowledge and better perspective, assured me my fears were groundless. But even then, I had to take him at his word. And that is how it is with God. Jesus promised the disciples, "After I have been raised, I *will go before you* to Galilee" – and He did (Matthew 26:32; italics added). Galilee was home for the disciples, but though it held many memories, it also raised fears. In that respect, each of us has his own particular "Galilee," some situation that poses a threat to us, whether real or imaginary. And although we cannot see Him, an omniscient Jesus with eternal perspective goes before us, and we receive the assurances we need when we take Him at His word.

Light: "He is not far from each one of us" (Acts 17:27).

Reflection: How close am I to God?

Birds of a Feather

You shall not be partial to the poor nor defer to the great.
Leviticus 19:15

Going about the kitchen during the course of the day, I seldom pause to observe the sparrows at the bird feeder. After all, if you've seen one sparrow, you've seen them all. The family rebukes me for even feeding them, but I suppose I harbor a certain pity for the poor things. They are such dull brown birds – and much maligned. Their presence is also a constant reminder of Matthew 10:31: "You are of more value than many sparrows." When self-esteem hits an all time low, such thoughts help, but not much.

Blue jays are different. In the presence of less majestic specimens of bird, they stand out crest and shoulders above the rest. Their irritable nature taken into consideration, however, they really have but one admirable quality.

Their plumage is impressive.

For that reason alone I find myself catering to their every whim and fancy. The sparrows have birdseed; the blue jays get sunflowers. The sparrows have bread crumbs; the blue jays get suet. Is it not worth the extra expense just to see such magnificent birds? Of course!

But wait a minute. Up to this point the sunflowers and suet were freewill offerings. Of late, however, their majesties the blue jays seem to think they *deserve* them. If such delicacies are not forthcoming they peer into the window and indignantly *demand* gratification.

Flamboyant and sophisticated they may appear, but I have come to realize that those blue jays also exhibit certain traits I have hitherto despised – greed, arrogance, conceit, and showmanship, to name a few. And here I am, accountable for fostering the attention of overbearing birdbrains who think it not the least bit improper to solicit support by virtue of appearances only.

Shame on me.

Influenced by the value system of the world in which we live, it is easy enough to "defer to the great" and pity the "plain Janes," to curry the favor of richly attired "blue jays" and overlook poorly dressed "sparrows." In the second chapter of the book of James there is a strong admonition to the church about catering to the social prestige of the wealthy while snubbing the poor. The writer points out that such tendencies among Christians are not only wrongly motivated, self-seeking and risky, but "if you show partiality, you are committing sin" (James 2:9).

Those are strong but timely words, for they jolt us into examining our attitudes toward the poor, the rich, the underprivileged, the fortunate, the plain, the beautiful, the old, the young, the failed, the successful. Try as we might, we cannot justify the acceptance of some and the exclusion of others and still claim to be impartial.

Light: "But the wisdom that is from above is first pure, then peaceable, gentle, and easy to be entreated, full of mercy and good fruits, without partiality, and without hypocrisy" (James 3:17).

Reflection: Do I exercise godly wisdom and value every person I meet, or do I pick and choose only those whom I admire?

The Empty Nest

*There was not one that flapped its
wing or opened its beak or chirped.*
Isaiah 10:14

A local educational center recently sponsored a
course called "The Empty Nest – An Opportunity to
Disassem-ble and Renew."

It was a catchy title, but for those of us who grew up
on farms, it brought to mind the plump old hens who
fussed and fumed at length over empty nests. Long after
the chicks had flown the coop, the hens were still
clucking about their plight. They were a highly irritable
lot, those old girls, and I am not sure I like to be identified
as one. At most, I will admit that it ruffles my feathers
when the experts imply that the transition to an empty
nest is virtually beyond the average mother.

Who finds it so difficult to cook less and linger longer
over a leisurely supper? No spilled milk, no juvenile

squabbles, no teenage smart cracks to belittle my leftovers – is that so hard to take?

No smelly gym socks to wash, no jeans to mend, no arguments about crazy, impractical fads – I can do without those as well and not feel deprived.

A telephone all to myself, a car with a full gas tank – such conveniences are not exactly crosses for the middle-aged woman to bear.

Neither do I entertain much self-pity because I am no longer afforded the pleasure of listening to the top ten on the radio, turned up full volume to compensate for my loss of hearing.

I admit I feel somewhat at a loss choosing my own TV program without so much as a murmur of protest. Finding the newspaper intact also takes a certain amount of adjustment. I keep wanting to round up the comics from the rec room, the sports from the bathroom, and the entertainment section from under somebody's bed.

Once settled in my easy chair, however, it is no great hardship not to be ejected out into a cold, dark night just because Junior needs a ride home from lessons. And if I decide to take a long, relaxing bath, I can actually find a dry towel, the bar of soap, and my very own shampoo exactly where I left it.

I assume I am going through the process of "disassembling and renewing." As such, it is not nearly the traumatic experience I had been warned about. But then, there is a difference between "disassembling" and simply falling apart, that difference being *preparation*.

Scripture has much to say about preparing ahead, of readying ourselves for everything from worship to work to witnessing. Children are not permanent fixtures in any home, and it is shortsighted of us to raise them with those expectations. Adjusting to the idea of their eventual departure from the nest, therefore, is a necessary preparation, both mentally and emotionally. Accepting the fact that God loves and cares for our offspring even more than we do makes it so much easier to let them go.

Light: "Like an eagle that stirs up its nest, that hovers over its young, He spread His wings and caught them. He carried them on His pinions" (Deuteronomy 32:11).

Reflection: Do I entrust my family daily to God's care, in the full assurance that He keeps them "under His wings"? (Psalm 91:4).

A Stitch in Time

There is an appointed time for everything ... A
time to tear apart, and a time to sew together.
Ecclesiastes 3:1,7

Whenever I unplug my sewing machine, the family's clothing seems to disintegrate before my eyes. The boys' pajamas suddenly resemble frayed dust rags, their knees eat through their pants like acid, and every shirt they own looks like Huckleberry Finn's hand-me-downs.

The bottom drops out of friend hubby's pockets, the zipper on his jacket hangs by one tooth, and the lining of his overcoat falls down, creating an unsightly flounce around the bottom.

Buttons drop like dead flies, straps snap, and elastic sags.

I compliment the girl on how nice she looks today, and she bursts into tears. "I do *not!* You're just saying that because you don't want to sew anymore. My skirt

117

is too long, and my blouse doesn't fit right, and my own mother doesn't even care!"

If I recall correctly, she said she didn't look right yesterday either, but that was because I insisted upon sewing all her clothes and other girls her age could wear "bought stuff."

I commend the teenager for cleaning out his closet in the interests of charity, and he promptly informs me that those are *not* castoffs. Either the seams are split, the pockets are dangling, or the knees are torn.

Staggering under the load, I force my way into the sewing room, very much aware that the magnitude of the task awaiting me is nothing more than the accumulated results of my own procrastination. The truth of the old saying "A stitch in time saves nine" fairly shouts at me from the pile of mending.

As I sit there working, it is with the realization that nobody can avoid the wear and tear of life, but we can be prompt about doing our mending. Damaged relationships, frayed nerves, and patience worn thin are all the results of our human weaknesses. Or perhaps our problem is "the cantankerous zipper syndrome" – when we open our mouth, it won't close. Or maybe we learn to our dismay that we are earning wages "to put into a purse with holes" (Haggai 1:6). Or like buttons that mysteriously disappear, "riches ... make themselves wings" (Proverbs 23:5, KJV).

The tendency in such situations is to let matters drag.

Like careless children, we tell ourselves that one little hole won't matter, one little rip won't show, one lost button is neither here nor there. One thing leads to another, however, until the prospects of patching up so many areas of life at once is as overwhelming as a huge pile of mending. Not only that, but what may have been a series of simple repair jobs is now much more complicated.

Whether it is in the area of broken relationships, lost priorities, or careless stewardship, Scripture exhorts us to be prompt about seeking forgiveness, restoring a proper value system, and exercising self-discipline. If so, we avoid the accumulated consequences of our own neglect, and God is able to help us mend our ways in much shorter time.

Light: "Thou sewest up mine iniquity" (Job 14:17, KJV).

Reflection: Father, thank You that You forgive me and help me patch up the holes in my testimony and the torn relationships in my walk.